MAKING MONEY ONLINE: BOOK 3

BY MICHAEL CALLUM MAYAKA

FREELANCING AND REMOTE WORK

FOREWORD:

In today's digital age, making money online has become a viable and accessible option for individuals seeking financial independence or additional income streams. The internet offers a plethora of opportunities that allow you to leverage your skills, creativity, and resources to generate revenue. This guide aims to provide you with valuable insights, strategies, and practical tips on how to make money online effectively.

This book is part of a series for more information see Further reading at the end of this book.

Table of Contents

Foreword: 3
3. Freelancing and Remote Work 5
   3.1 Identifying Marketable Skills 6
   3.2 Platforms for Freelancers 12
      1. Upwork: 13
      2. Fiverr: 13
      3. Freelancer: 14
      4. Toptal: 15
      5. Guru: 16
      6. PeoplePerHour: 17
   3.3 Building a Portfolio and Attracting Clients 19
      1. Define your niche and target audience: 19
      2. Showcase your best work: 20
      3. Provide case studies and testimonials: 21
      4. Create a visually appealing portfolio: 22
      5. Optimize your online presence: 22
      6. Network and seek referrals: 23
      7. Market yourself effectively: 24
      8. Provide excellent customer service: 25
   3.4 Remote Job Opportunities: Embracing the Freedom of Work from Anywhere 27
      1. Remote Jobs in Information Technology (IT): 28
      2. Remote Jobs in Customer Service and Support: 29
      3. Remote Jobs in Marketing and Digital Media: 30
      4. Remote Jobs in Education and Online Tutoring: 31
      5. Remote Jobs in Project Management and Consulting: 32
Further reading: 35

3. FREELANCING AND REMOTE WORK

3.1 IDENTIFYING MARKETABLE SKILLS

In the ever-evolving job market, it is crucial to possess marketable skills that set you apart from the competition and open up opportunities for professional growth and financial success. Marketable skills are those that are in high demand, align with industry trends, and are sought after by employers and clients. Here are some essential steps to help you identify and develop your marketable skills:

1. Self-Assessment: Begin by conducting a thorough self-assessment to identify your strengths, passions, and areas of expertise. Reflect on your educational background, work

experience, hobbies, and personal interests. Consider the skills you enjoy using and excel in, as well as those that have received positive feedback from others. This introspection will help you uncover your unique abilities and potential areas for skill development.

2. Industry Research: Stay up to date with industry trends and the skills that are in demand. Research the job market and analyze job postings, career websites, and professional forums to identify the skills employers are seeking. Additionally, reach out to professionals in your desired field and engage in conversations about the skills that have helped them succeed. This research will provide valuable insights into the specific skills

that can make you marketable in your chosen industry.

3. Transferable Skills: While industry-specific skills are important, don't overlook transferable skills that can be valuable across various sectors. These skills include communication, problem-solving, leadership, teamwork, time management, and adaptability. Assess your transferable skills and consider how they can be applied to different roles or industries. Highlighting these skills can make you a versatile candidate and increase your marketability.

4. Skill Gap Analysis: Identify any gaps between your current skill set and the skills

required in your target industry. This analysis will help you prioritize which skills to develop and invest in. Consider taking courses, attending workshops, or pursuing certifications to acquire the necessary knowledge and expertise. Online learning platforms, industry-specific training programs, and professional associations can be excellent resources for acquiring new skills.

5. Emerging Skills: Keep an eye on emerging technologies, trends, and innovative practices within your industry. New technologies and advancements can create demand for specific skills. Stay informed through industry publications, online forums, webinars, and conferences. By being an early adopter of

emerging skills, you can position yourself as a valuable asset in a rapidly evolving market.

6. Feedback and Networking: Seek feedback from mentors, colleagues, and industry professionals who can provide insights into your strengths and areas for improvement. Engage in networking activities to expand your professional connections and gain exposure to new opportunities. Networking can also help you identify skills that are highly valued within your professional community.

Remember that identifying marketable skills is an ongoing process. As industries evolve and new demands emerge, you must continuously assess and update your skill set. Adaptability, a willingness to learn, and a growth mindset are essential traits for staying marketable in a rapidly changing job market. By consistently honing your skills, you will enhance your professional prospects and increase your chances of success in the competitive landscape of today's workforce.

3.2 PLATFORMS FOR FREELANCERS

In the realm of online work, freelancing has gained significant popularity as a flexible and accessible way to earn income. Freelancers offer their skills and services to clients on a project-by-project basis, allowing them to work independently and on their own terms. To connect freelancers with potential clients, numerous online platforms have emerged, providing a marketplace for freelancers to showcase their expertise and find work opportunities. In this section, we will explore some of the top platforms for freelancers.

1. UPWORK:

Upwork is one of the most well-known and widely used platforms for freelancers. It offers a wide range of job categories, including writing, web development, graphic design, marketing, and more. Upwork allows freelancers to create a profile, highlight their skills and experience, and bid on projects posted by clients. The platform also provides tools for time tracking, communication, and secure payment processing.

2. FIVERR:

Fiverr is a platform that focuses on micro-jobs or gigs. Freelancers on Fiverr offer services in various categories, such as writing, graphic design, voiceover, video editing, and social media management. Instead of bidding on projects, freelancers create "gigs" with predefined services and prices. Clients can browse through these gigs and hire freelancers directly. Fiverr emphasizes quick turnaround times and affordable services, making it suitable for freelancers starting out or offering specialized skills.

3. FREELANCER:

Freelancer.com is another popular platform that connects freelancers with clients worldwide. It offers a diverse range of job categories, including programming, design, writing, marketing, and more. Freelancers can create a profile, showcase their work, and bid on projects posted by clients. Freelancer also features contests, where freelancers can participate and submit their work for a chance to win the project. The platform provides tools for communication, milestone-based payments, and dispute resolution.

4. TOPTAL:

Toptal is a platform dedicated to connecting freelancers with high-quality clients in the field of software development, design, and finance. Toptal takes a rigorous screening process to ensure the freelancers on their platform are top-tier professionals. Instead of bidding, Toptal matches freelancers with clients based on their skills and requirements. This platform offers higher-paying opportunities and focuses on long-term projects with established companies and startups.

5. GURU:

Guru is a platform that offers a wide range of job categories, including programming, writing, design, marketing, and more. Freelancers can create a profile, showcase their work, and bid on projects posted by clients. Guru features a workroom where freelancers and clients can collaborate, share files, and track progress. The platform also provides a built-in invoicing and payment system, making it convenient for freelancers to manage their projects and finances.

6. PEOPLEPERHOUR:

PeoplePerHour is a platform that caters to freelancers specializing in web development, design, writing, marketing, and other creative fields. Freelancers can create a profile, define their hourly rates, and showcase their portfolios. Clients can browse freelancers' profiles and hire them based on their expertise and availability. PeoplePerHour also offers a WorkStream feature for smooth project management, communication, and invoicing.

These platforms serve as intermediaries between freelancers and clients, providing a streamlined process for finding work opportunities, securing projects, and facilitating payments. Each platform has its own unique features, pricing structure, and user base. It's essential for freelancers to carefully choose the platforms that align with their skills, goals, and target clients. By leveraging these platforms effectively, freelancers can access a vast network of potential clients, expand their professional network, and build a successful freelance career.

3.3 BUILDING A PORTFOLIO AND ATTRACTING CLIENTS

In the world of online freelancing and remote work, having a strong portfolio is essential for attracting clients and showcasing your skills and expertise. A portfolio serves as a visual representation of your work and acts as a testament to your capabilities. In this section, we will explore the steps involved in building an impressive portfolio and attracting clients to your online services.

1. DEFINE YOUR NICHE AND TARGET AUDIENCE:

Before you start building your portfolio, it's important to identify your niche and target audience. Determine the specific services you want to offer and the type of clients you want to work with. Having a clear focus will help you tailor your portfolio to showcase relevant samples and attract the right clients who are seeking your particular skills.

2. SHOWCASE YOUR BEST WORK:

When it comes to building a portfolio, quality matters more than quantity. Select a few samples that represent your best work and align with the services you offer. These samples should demonstrate your expertise, creativity, and problem-solving abilities. Include a variety of projects to showcase your versatility, but ensure that they are cohesive and reflective of your niche.

3. PROVIDE CASE STUDIES AND TESTIMONIALS:

To add depth and credibility to your portfolio, consider including case studies or success stories that highlight the challenges you faced and how you overcame them. This provides potential clients with valuable insights into your problem-solving abilities and the results you can achieve. Additionally, including testimonials or client reviews can build trust and showcase your professionalism.

4. CREATE A VISUALLY APPEALING PORTFOLIO:

Design and presentation play a crucial role in attracting clients to your portfolio. Ensure that your portfolio has an organized and visually appealing layout. Use high-quality images, clear descriptions, and an intuitive navigation system. A visually cohesive and professional portfolio will leave a lasting impression on potential clients.

5. OPTIMIZE YOUR ONLINE PRESENCE:

In addition to having a dedicated portfolio website, it's important to establish a strong online presence to attract clients. Create profiles on relevant freelancing platforms, professional networking sites, and social media platforms. Optimize your profiles with relevant keywords, showcase your portfolio samples, and actively engage with potential clients and industry peers. This will help you increase your visibility and connect with potential clients.

6. NETWORK AND SEEK REFERRALS:

Networking is a powerful tool for attracting clients. Attend industry-related events, join online communities, and actively engage with professionals in your field. Build relationships with influencers and thought leaders, as they can potentially refer clients to you. Actively seek referrals from satisfied clients and use their positive feedback to showcase your capabilities to new clients.

7. MARKET YOURSELF EFFECTIVELY:

Don't shy away from self-promotion. Develop a strong personal brand and create compelling marketing materials such as a professional website, blog, or newsletter. Utilize content marketing strategies to demonstrate your expertise and provide value to your target audience. Collaborate with other professionals, guest post on relevant websites, and participate in industry discussions to increase your visibility and attract clients.

8. PROVIDE EXCELLENT CUSTOMER SERVICE:

Satisfied clients are more likely to refer you to others and become repeat customers. Focus on delivering exceptional customer service by promptly responding to inquiries, delivering projects on time, and exceeding client expectations. Your reputation for providing excellent service will spread, attracting more clients to your portfolio.

In conclusion, building a portfolio and attracting clients in the online space requires strategic planning, showcasing your best work, creating a visually appealing portfolio, optimizing your online presence, networking, effective marketing, and providing excellent customer service. By following these steps and continuously refining your portfolio and client attraction strategies, you will be well on your way to establishing a successful online presence and attracting clients to your services.

3.4 REMOTE JOB OPPORTUNITIES: EMBRACING THE FREEDOM OF WORK FROM ANYWHERE

In recent years, the concept of remote work has gained significant traction, offering individuals the freedom and flexibility to work from the comfort of their own homes or any location of their choosing. Remote job opportunities have become increasingly popular, enabling professionals to escape the confines of traditional office settings and embrace a more flexible work-life balance. This section explores the growing landscape of remote job opportunities and highlights the benefits and challenges they present.

Remote work offers a diverse range of opportunities across various industries and sectors. Companies are recognizing the advantages of remote teams, including reduced overhead costs, access to a global talent pool, and improved employee satisfaction. As a result, the number of remote job listings has grown exponentially, providing individuals with a wide array of choices.

1. REMOTE JOBS IN INFORMATION TECHNOLOGY (IT):

The IT industry is at the forefront of remote work, with many roles suitable for remote employees. Software development, web design, cybersecurity, data analysis, and technical support are just a few examples of IT positions that can be performed remotely. Professionals in this field can enjoy the freedom to work for global companies or even start their own remote IT consulting businesses.

2. REMOTE JOBS IN CUSTOMER SERVICE AND SUPPORT:

Customer service and support roles have also adapted to the remote work trend. Many companies hire remote customer service representatives, chat support agents, and virtual assistants to handle customer inquiries and provide support remotely. These roles often require excellent communication skills, problem-solving abilities, and the ability to work independently.

3. REMOTE JOBS IN MARKETING AND DIGITAL MEDIA:

The digital era has created numerous remote job opportunities in the field of marketing and digital media. Remote positions such as social media managers, content writers, digital marketers, SEO specialists, and graphic designers are in high demand. These roles allow professionals to collaborate with teams, manage campaigns, and create engaging content from anywhere in the world.

4. REMOTE JOBS IN EDUCATION AND ONLINE TUTORING:

The education sector has also embraced remote work, particularly in online tutoring and e-learning platforms. Remote teaching positions, course development, instructional design, and language tutoring are among the opportunities available. Online tutoring enables educators to connect with students worldwide, fostering cross-cultural exchange and expanding access to education.

5. REMOTE JOBS IN PROJECT MANAGEMENT AND CONSULTING:

Project managers and consultants can also enjoy remote work opportunities. With the aid of project management tools and communication platforms, professionals can lead and oversee projects remotely, collaborating with teams and clients regardless of geographical boundaries. Remote consulting offers opportunities in areas such as business strategy, human resources, marketing, and finance.

While remote job opportunities offer numerous advantages, they also come with unique challenges. Communication and collaboration can be more complex when team members are spread across different time zones and locations. Additionally, remote work requires discipline, self-motivation, and the ability to manage time effectively to ensure productivity and work-life balance.

To find remote job opportunities, various websites and platforms specialize in listing remote positions, such as Remote.co, FlexJobs, and Upwork. Networking and building a strong online presence through professional platforms like LinkedIn can also increase visibility and connect individuals with remote job opportunities.

In conclusion, remote job opportunities have revolutionized the way people work, providing the freedom to choose their location while pursuing meaningful and rewarding careers. As technology continues to advance, the remote work landscape will only expand, creating more opportunities for professionals across diverse industries. Embracing remote work can lead to increased flexibility, improved work-life balance, and the ability to unlock your full potential while exploring new horizons.

FURTHER READING:

If you enjoyed this book, please consider reading one of the other books in the series:

Making Money Online: Book 1 (Understanding the Online Landscape)

Making Money Online: Book 2 (E-commerce and Online Retail)

Making Money Online: Book 3 (Freelancing and Remote Work)

Making Money Online: Book 4 (Content Creation and Monetization)

Making Money Online: Book 5 (Online Tutoring and Education)

Making Money Online: Book 6 (Online Surveys, Microtasks, and Rewards)

Making Money Online: Book 7 (Online Investments and Trading)

Making Money Online: Book 8 (Creating and Selling Digital Assets)

Making Money Online: Book 9 (Online Consulting and Coaching)

Making Money Online: Book 10 (Maximizing Online Income Opportunities)

All the books can be found on Amazon as Kindle and Paperback, or you can buy the complete edition which contains the full series in one book. The complete edition is available as Kindle, Paperback and exclusively as Hardback. You can find all the links in my book site: books.michaelmayaka.co.uk.